GOTHIC GARGOYLES

GOTHIC GARGOYLES

TEXT AND PHOTOGRAPHY BY

BILL YENNE

BARNES
&NOBLE
BOOKS
NEW YORK

This edition published by
Barnes & Noble, Inc., by arrangement
with O.G. Publishing, Inc.

2000 Barnes & Noble Books

Produced by
American Graphic Systems, Inc.
PO Box 460313
San Francisco, CA 94146
Fax: (415) 285-8790

Design © 1998
American Graphic Systems, Inc.

M 10 9 8 7 6 5 4 3 2 1

ISBN 0-7607-2285-4

Printed in China

All photographs were taken by the author
and are
© 1998 William P. Yenne
except those on pages 110 and 111,
which are by Thomas-Photos Oxford,
and were supplied through the courtesy
of APS Masonry of Oxford, England

Designed by Bill Yenne with design
assistance from Azia Yenne.
Proofreading by Joan B. Hayes
and Amy Bokser.

The author would like to extend a special thanks to everyone who helped make this book possible, especially Carol Yenne, Geert Govaert of Westvlaamse Gidsenkring, Paul Maeyaert, Liliane Opsomer of the Belgian Tourist Office, Herman Vermeulen of Voorzitter Gidsenbond, Line Vervoordeldonk of Kring Vrienden and last, but never least, to my friend Todd Siemers for his work in translating valuable original source materials.

The photographs at the front of this book were taken at the following locations:
Page one:
Palais de Justice, Rouen, France
Pages 2-3:
Notre Dame de Paris (south tower),
Paris, France
Pages 4-5:
Notre Dame d'Amiens (north tower),
Amiens, France
Pages 6-7 (these pages):
Notre Dame de Paris (north tower)
Pages 8-9:
Palais de Justice, Rouen, France

Notes on dates:
Because no records were kept in regard to when Gothic gargoyles were originally carved, the centuries noted in this book are our best guess estimates, based on when the specific building or section thereof, was built.

In some cases, two centuries are noted. For example, the towers at Notre Dame de Paris were built in the thirteenth century, but were extensively restored in the nineteenth century; the cathedral in Cologne was completed in the nineteenth century, but damaged and restored in the twentieth century, and so on.

TABLE OF CONTENTS

PREFACE

. . . .

ARGOYLES fire our imaginations because they are mysterious — yet tangible — artifacts from the past that are clues to another world which we cannot fully understand. There is something in human nature that loves a mystery. People are fascinated by the unknown and the ethereal.

This book is the result of a personal experience spanning three decades, a mere moment in the virtually timeless history of gargoyles, but a large part of my life. It began in the spring of 1969 in John Stocking's Art History 235 class at the University of Montana, and ended (for the purposes of this book) amid the sandstone canyons and the flying buttresses high atop the Cathedral of St. Rombout in Mechelen, Belgium. Over the years, I have visited gargoyles throughout Europe and North America, especially those who live on the great cathedrals that typify the art and architecture of the Gothic period.

Gargoyles are tangible. We know their *where* and *when*. Yet they are also mysterious, because we cannot

▲

Gothic Revival Gargoyle
Madison Avenue at East 29th Street
New York City, USA
(Northwest corner)
Nineteenth Century
. . . .

be sure of their *what*, *why*, and *who*. In many — but not all — cases, we can tell *what* they are intended to represent, but in most cases we don't know *why*. The people who attempt to answer this question are guessing. Those who know have been dead for eight centuries. This is why the *who* is especially fascinating to me. I was also taking a sculpture class in that spring of 1969, and spent a lot of time thinking about those medieval sculptors, and about who they were.

We can see gargoyles at a distance while standing on the ground, but if we climb in search of them, we find ourselves in a very different place: this is where the medieval sculptors, masons and builders had climbed. From a distance, we are certainly awed by the beauty of these vast Gothic buildings. They are at once massive and delicate, simultaneously deep in shadow and bathed in radiant light. But up close, we get a humbling feel for the craftsmanship that made them possible. In reflecting on how long these buildings have survived, and on the tools that were available to build them, we can only come away with a deep respect for those who designed, built and embellished the grand monuments of the Middle Ages. Pausing alone at a slit window in a narrow passageway, 500 steps above the ground, one cannot help but think of those who were here first and those who lifted, placed and carved these massive stones. If we can get close enough to touch a gargoyle, and we usually can't, they are as hard and cold as paving stones. Yet, as we find ourselves in *their* world, high above our own, they seem much more real and much more — as their sculptors may have intended — alive.

To get close, you will have climbed a narrow tunnel, walked a narrow walkway, balanced on a narrow parapet, and you will be very far from having your feet firmly on the ground. You are out of your world and in theirs. You work to maintain balance, both physically and in your perception of your surroundings. Things are different up here, and that is probably what the builders had in mind. The buttresses and spires are all around you, reaching high above,

Rooster-Griffin
Notre Dame d'Evreux
Evreux, France
(Exterior, south ambulatory)
Thirteenth Century

disappearing far below, crossing above your head and blocking your way. The sounds of the street below are distant, far away, and lost in the sound of the wind. The houses and cars are just specks, but only if you look down, and you really don't want to look down.

The sandstone upper reaches of the Gothic cathedrals are like the sandstone canyons of the American Southwest. You climb amid stone formations that are hard and immobile, but at the same time, you find them amazingly organic and fluid in their appearance.

You move carefully, not wanting to slip and fall, and not knowing exactly what you'll find around the next corner. You reach for a handhold, catch your breath and glance up at the structure soaring above. You have climbed very high, but still higher there are strange creatures perched on spindly pinnacles. Some seem to be ignoring you, but others are looking directly at you. As you glance away, you detect a flicker of movement out of the corner of your eye.

— *Bill Yenne*

INTRODUCTION

. . . .

IN THE great cities of Europe, the home of our Western classical sculptural heritage, people marvel at floodlit Donatellos, splendidly exhibited Michelangelos, and the wonderful statues that adorn the majestic cathedrals. But as the sun sets, another breed of beast, the product of the hand of a different sort of sculptor, comes into its hour. They sit as they have for as long as eight centuries, and peer down anonymously at the sleeping European cities and towns.

The Gothic gargoyles frighten and intrigue us in the same way that the creatures from horror and science fiction movies simultaneously frighten and intrigue us. They were created as much as eight centuries before either of those genres reached the silver screen, but far from dating them, their age is part of the mystery and mythology of gargoyles. It has served to make them a timeless part of our collective heritage. The gargoyles were created long ago by craftsmen

Gargoyle with Bulging Eyes
Hôtel de Ville
Brussels, Belgium
(North facade)
Fifteenth/Nineteenth Centuries

▶

Gargoyle Rookery
Notre Dame de Paris
Paris, France
(South tower)
Thirteenth/Nineteenth Centuries

. . . .

whose names and motives were long ago lost to the sands of time. Any explanation of their fearsome iconography is pure conjecture. Though many have enjoyed varying degrees of restoration, most gargoyles are very old.

They were also created over a broad span of time. Most of the great cathedrals that typify the Gothic style were constructed between the twelfth and fifteenth centuries, with many of them taking more than a century to build. They were among the largest and most complex buildings yet to be constructed, and many architectural innovations, from arches to flying buttresses, were either invented or refined in order to accomplish the truly monumental task of completing cathedrals and to carrying the enormous weight of these buildings. In addition to the grand and massive features of the cathedrals was a myriad of smaller details, which included the gargoyles.

In the nineteenth century, European and American architects

and historians rediscovered and proceeded to thoroughly study the art and architecture of Gothic cathedrals, churches, and public buildings. Many scholarly and popular works have been published on this subject, but while many of them go into minute detail on other topics, they usually ignore gargoyles, or merely mention them in passing. In the early nineteenth century, anything that was the least bit tainted with the demonic or the pagan was considered inappropriate for polite dialogue at best, or downright evil at the extreme.

As time went on, gargoyles came to be considered merely trivial. Their iconography was unimportant because it was indecipherable. Most gargoyles were also dozens, or even hundreds, of feet above the ground. They were hard to see and easy to forget. Why they had flourished remained a mystery. The gargoyle sculptors — who, like most people at the time, were probably illiterate — left no written records. They left only their work.

What Are Gargoyles?

WHEN those sculptors finished this work, what *did* they leave? Gargoyles are, first and foremost, water spouts. In Harris & Lever's *Illustrated Glossary of Architecture*, gargoyles are simply defined as "spouts in the form of a carved grotesque human or animal head projecting

Copper-lined Human Gargoyle
Sainte-Chapelle
Paris, France
(Apse)
Thirteenth Century

from the top of a wall, to throw off rainwater." Indeed, the word is derived from the French word *gargouille*, which literally means "water spout."

The similarly fantastic creatures on cathedrals and public buildings that are more nearly flush to the surface and do not throw off rainwater are properly referred to in architectural terms as "grotesques," although, in popular parlance, they too are "gargoyles."

Of course, not all water spouts on medieval buildings take the form of fantastic beasts, and many gargoyles that are carved in the shapes of beasts are carved in the shapes of real animals, or at least caricatures of real animals. But it is the fantastic that inspires our imagination, and it is the fantastic that is the focus of the present work.

From where did the idea for fantastic gargoyles and grotesques come? Water spouts in the shape of animals existed in the ancient Mediterranean area in both the Greek and Etruscan civilizations, and they were borrowed by Roman architects. However, the presence of entire rookeries of fantastic hybrid monsters began in with the dawn of the Gothic period in architecture with the beginning of the era of the great cathedrals.

Just as the creatures themselves were usually hybrids, their origin was probably an amalgam of Roman architectural style and the dragons of ancient Celtic mythology. The gargoyles probably originated in

Hybrid Gargoyles with a Woman
Notre Dame d'Amiens
Amiens, France
(South facade)
Fourteenth Century

the twelfth century in northern France, where real and imaginary animals had been an important element of architectural decoration since the beginning of the Romanesque period in the tenth century.

Constructed roughly simultaneously, the great cathedrals at Chartres, Rouen, and Paris are a testimony to the sudden population explosion of these amazing creatures. Within a century, the gargoyles had migrated to what is now Belgium and the Netherlands, and to England, Germany and Italy.

Because gargoyles are water spouts that extend from the sides of buildings, they are usually long-necked, with the head being at the outermost end, although a few gargoyles have the opposite end of the animal extended. They vary in length from about 18 inches to more than four feet. Some are ramrod straight, while others are slightly curved. Occasionally, such as at Louviers in Normandy, one will encounter a two-headed gargoyle, with the two necks curving away from the shoulders at different angles. Most, though certainly not all, gargoyles are composed of an entire body rather than simply the shoulders, neck and head.

In Gothic churches, gargoyles and grotesques may occur almost anywhere, but they are usually found in certain architectural sections. If there are gargoyles at all, there is often a row of them on the outside walls of the nave, or the sides of the main part of the building. These are usually located outside the clerestory, or wall of stained glass windows; often, but not always, at the top of the rectangular part of the window near its arched top. These will be located roughly 20 to 30 feet above the ground (or at both heights), and there is usually a gargoyle between each pair of windows. Grotesques may also be present, but because they are usually closer to being flush with the face of the structure, they will not be as prominent as the gargoyles, which jut out.

The pattern of gargoyles (and/or grotesques) on the exterior of the nave is generally repeated on the facades of the wings of the transept — if the transept extends far enough from the nave of the church — and gargoyles almost certainly recur on the exterior facade of the ambulatory that runs around the rear, or apse, of the church. It might be noted that this part of the church usually faces east and is the first to catch the rays of the morning sun, and the first to be bathed in evening shadow.

Gargoyle Rookery
Notre Dame d'Amiens
Amiens, France
(South facade)
Fourteenth Century
. . . .

Above these rows of gargoyles there may be a second row, about 20 to 30 feet above the first, near the base of the roof, and/or on the sides of the abutments, where the flying buttresses terminate.

On the facade of the church, gargoyles are less likely to occur lower than 30 feet above the ground, and not in a way as to interfere with the triforia above the main doors. Grotesques may occur as low as eye-level, but if so, they are usually tucked into a crevice or corner.

Gargoyles — often very large ones — occur frequently at the tops of towers, usually at each of the four corners. Gargoyles will also be found at the base, and often at the waist, of the spire if there is one. The larger size of the higher gargoyles may have to do with their distance from the ground and a desire to make them more visible, although this theory runs contrary to the popular notion that gargoyles are intended to be hard to see. Like so many things about gargoyles, this, too, is part of their mystery.

As with the other statuary on the Gothic churches of Europe, most gargoyles produced during the twelfth through the fifteenth centuries were carved of Brabantine sandstone, and the larger ones were reinforced with iron bars that are generally one to two inches in diameter. During the nineteenth century restorations, French limestone was generally used as a mater-

Army of Gargoyles
Notre Dame de Paris
Paris, France
(Exterior, south ambulatory)
Twelfth Century
. . . .

ial. Because the iron was prone to rusting and deterioration over time, copper came into use in the nineteenth century for reinforcing the larger gargoyles. In the twentieth century, stainless steel was used. One can imagine the gargoyle sculptor at work, alone and high above the rest of his fellow workers; but in fact, most of the gargoyles were probably carved on the ground and lifted into place along with other materials and components.

Gargoyles were carved with hammer and chisel and finished with various abrasives. They were not cast in molds using mortar. Because they were used as water spouts, most had a groove, or channel, that ran the length of their spine, terminating at the head. In a few cases, a metal (often copper, but probably originally lead) trough was used to line the groove. In some cases, such metal covered the back of the neck and occasionally the back of the head. In more than half of all gargoyles, the water spills off the top of the head, but many have a hole drilled through the head so that the water spills through the open mouth.

Gargoyles were usually carved from the same block of stone as the structural piece to which they are attached, so gargoyle-carving was probably very much a part of the construction process of the cathedral, rather than being an afterthought or embellishment that came later. Because of their height, they would have been added in the latter half of the construction process, but the gargoyles on a given building are likely to have been carved over a span of many years, or even several decades.

Gargoyles are an integral part of the decorative aesthetic of Gothic architecture. As art historian Paul Frankl wrote, "The multitude of decorative detail and the gargoyles vitalize both the horizontal and vertical lines."

Explaining Gargoyles

SINCE no records have survived through the centuries from the years when they were first carved, interpretations of gargoyles can only be inferred. The Victorian scholars who embraced the Gothic Revival either ignored the idea of an interpretation of the gargoyles and grotesques, or dismissed the gargoyles as the product of demonology or nightmares. Even in the twentieth century, very little work has been done on gargoyles by art historians. There have been many works on the complex iconography of

Dragon Grotesque
Notre Dame de Chartres
Chartres, France
(North tower)
Thirteenth Century

medieval painting and sculpture, but very little has been written on the iconography of gargoyles. Indeed, there is no accepted explanation of why they exist as they do.

Most interpretations see them as representing either Christian or pagan ideals. Some see them as a struggle between pagan and Christian, but they can also be seen as a harmony between the Christian and the pagan.

Gargoyles may be characters in the struggle between good and evil, which was once synonymous with the idea of Christian versus pagan. While the strict separation of Christian and pagan was probably not part of twelfth or thirteenth century thinking, by the nineteenth century, "pagan" would have certainly embraced such adjectives as "evil" and "satanic."

Biblical passages have been cited as possible sources for images of gargoyles. In the Middle Ages, with illiteracy the norm and books virtually unavailable, visual interpretations of scripture — in paintings and sculpture — were essential, and quite common. Among the passages that may have inspired gargoyles are those found in chapter seven of the Book of Daniel, in Psalm XXII, and in the Book of Revelation.

In Psalm XXII, David writes, "Many bulls of Bashan surround me; they open wide their mouths at me, like a ravening and roaring lion. . . . Yea, dogs are

Gargoyle Rookery
Church of Sainte-Waudru
Mons, Belgium
(Exterior, south ambulatory)
Seventeenth Century

around me; a company of evildoers encircles me." In the Book of Revelation, John reports seeing several fearsome hybrid monsters, especially multi-headed dragons.

Other interpreters see gargoyles as sort of spiritual scarecrows, intended to scare away the devil with a taste of his own gruesomeness. Ask anyone associated today with a medieval cathedral to explain their gargoyles, and the reply will often be a reference to keeping the rainwater as far away from the building as possible, as though the rainwater itself symbolizes evil.

Then too, the gargoyles may be representations of the fall of the rebel angels, demons forever condemned to the outside of the great cathedrals, and never allowed to enter the sanctified interior. This would explain the almost total lack of similar hybrid figures in the interior of cathedrals, but it would not explain the gargoyles on the exteriors of non-sanctified buildings.

While gargoyles may have been written off as evil in the nineteenth and early twentieth centuries because paganism was considered "bad," during the Middle

Ages, paganism was not bad, it was just part of the roots and traditions of everyday life. As missionaries brought Christianity to Northern Europe, they consciously grafted Christian symbolism onto pre-existing pagan beliefs. When St. Patrick brought Christianity to Ireland in the fifth century, he created the Celtic cross. In this symbol, a cross is superimposed on the ancient pagan circular device that represents the sun, as well as the unity and the totality of the universe. As such, it is a symbol not unlike the familiar Taoist yin yang. It could very well be that gargoyles, like the Celtic cross, have their roots in a blend of pagan mythology with Christian symbols, literature, and traditions.

In his book *Le Symbolisme Médiéval de la Statuaire de Notre-Dame d'Evreux*, an important work on medieval symbolism, Louis Aubert points out the strong pagan underpinnings of medieval culture. He notes that there was a strong interest in hermeticism, alchemy, and the occult, and a pervasive belief that the earth was the center of a cosmological universe in which God and nature reigned in omniscience. Out of these pagan beliefs came the notion that matter, mind, and spirit return to a primordial unity with God and the universe. Today, pagan beliefs are seen through a less jaundiced eye as

▲
Gargoyle in a Pinnacle
Notre Dame d'Evreux
Evreux, France
(Buttress pinnacle, south side)
Thirteenth Century

▶
Rooster-Griffin
Notre Dame d'Evreux
Evreux, France
(Exterior, south ambulatory)
Thirteenth Century
· · · · · · · · · · · · · · · · ·

just part of the "old ways" of pre-Christian nature religions. Nature was a comfortable fit with theology. The mysteries of nature that the pagans held in reverence were the work of an omnipotent creator whom the Christian missionaries identified in their monotheism as a single God. The divine power that pagans saw in nature was identified by Christianity as the Holy Spirit, of the three aspects of the Holy Trinity.

This pagan undercurrent was reflected in the art of the period more strongly than we generally realize. It is to be found in manuscript illumination, occasionally in the two-dimensional art of the Middle Ages, and high in the uppermost reaches of the great cathedrals, where peasant craftsmen, hired to carve decoration, rendered the strange and mysterious beasts that we know as the gargoyles.

Although the Council of Nice in 787 AD insisted that the composition of statues on churches be determined by Church authorities, not craftsmen, gargoyles were obviously accepted and sanctioned. Nevertheless, they were not universally understood and appreciated by the bishops and the established hierarchy within the Church. Louis Aubert reminds us that as early as 1125, while gargoyles were still being carved throughout northern France, St. Bernard — a

scholar and theologian of note — wrote a letter to the abbot at Abbaye St. Thierry complaining of what he described as "all these grotesque monsters. . . unclean apes and a single head attached to several bodies."

St. Bernard went on to ask rhetorically, "Of what use in the cloisters, under the eyes of the brothers during their pious readings, are these ridiculous monstrosities?" Nearly nine centuries later, we are asking the same question, although we now find them much more intriguing than ridiculous.

The sociological context of the times is also somewhat important in considering the demonic nature of gargoyles. Part of the reason that the Middle Ages were called the Dark Ages was that the day-to-day life of the average person was quite grim. Conditions in the cities — and many of the great cathedrals were being built in the cities — were miserable. Over-crowding, combined with poor sanitation, would have been bad enough, but it also led to disease, the causes of which were little understood at the time. The Middle Ages were, in fact, marred by rampant disease, with European society being in the grip of an epidemic — or, at the minimum, a bad flu season — almost continuously for centuries.

Anyone with a bad case of the flu — or worse — *feels* possessed by demons, and in the Middle Ages, peo-

▲

Crouching Gargoyle
Notre Dame de Paris
Paris, France
(North side door jamb)
Twelfth Century

. . . .

ple had no real notion that they *weren't* possessed by demons. Substitute the word "virus" for "demon" and these people were right. Even today, our cartoon depictions of both viruses and demons are clearly quite similar to the images of Gothic gargoyles. As a footnote to considering the effect of disease on the symbolism used gargoyle sculptors and other medieval artists, we should recall that the darkest moment of the Dark Ages came a the mid-point of the era of the Gothic cathedrals. Between 1348 and 1350, the Black Death — the dreaded bubonic plague epidemic — killed a third of the population of Europe.

Food poisoning may also have played a more important role than we could imagine. The horrible — even deadly — cramps were bad enough, but when the poison was ergot mold, the consequences verged on what may be described as worse than death. Ergot, which forms on rye bread in rare circumstances, contains lysergic acid, the active ingredient in the notorious hallucinogenic drug LSD. In the 1950s, a rural town in France suffered an outbreak of ergot poisoning in which some people were driven to suicide and insanity from their powerful hallucinations, especially including visions of monsters and strange hybrid animals. This incident is vividly described in John Grant Fuller's book *The Day of St. Anthony's Fire*.

Gargoyle Rookery

Notre Dame d''Amiens

Amiens, France

(Apse)

Fourteenth Century

· · · · · · · · · · · · · · · · ·

Because of the state of sanitation during the Middle Ages, ergot poisoning is thought to have been widespread. The terrible visions experienced by the survivors may have influenced a belief in the reality of monsters and hybrid creatures. Ergot poisoning, as well as other then-inexplicable maladies such as St. Vitus's Dance, also encouraged the long-standing belief in demonic possession, and, of course, in the demons themselves.

In attempting to intuit meaning by getting inside the mind of the gargoyle sculptor, there may be a ten-dency to focus too much on the symbolic and the metaphysical. Certainly these considerations play a big role in Gothic architecture, but in considering the revolutionary craftsmanship that went into building the great cathedrals, not to mention the craftsmen themselves, we are reminded that these were people of science — at least of the mathematical and engineering sciences — more than they were mystics and theoreticians.

During the halcyon days of Freudian and Jungian psychoanalysis in the mid-twentieth century, gargoyles were explained as manifestations of the sculptors' subconscious, and this may, in fact, have played a small part in some of the details.

One of the stranger notions suggested as an explanation for gargoyles was that they were based on unearthed dinosaur bones. However, it is relatively certain that people in the Dark Ages were still in the dark about what dinosaurs really looked like, and by the twelfth century, no full dinosaur skeletons had yet been assembled.

For those who interpreted a darker meaning, the gargoyles and grotesques were expressions of demonic cultists who managed to slip the monsters past the ecclesiastical censors. Given the time and manpower that was required to carve and install the gargoyles, this is improbable. It would have involved a cabal of truly massive proportions, and, despite the fringe cults that were known to exist in medieval Europe, there is no clear evidence for such a conspiracy.

The most plausible explanation for the nature of gargoyles is that the sculptors who invented them probably became bored with carving leaves and scrolls, and pulled the gargoyles not from bad dreams, but from their rich imaginations and folklore. Like the larger saints and religious figures that are more prominently placed in and around Gothic churches, the gargoyles illustrate stories, historical or mythological.

It has been said that the great cathedrals were books in stone, and indeed they may well be encyclopedias of medieval doctrine, ecclesiastical, secular, satirical, mystic, and even occult. The stained glass windows tell their story, as do the sculptures that fill the triforium galleries above the doorways and the magnificent statues around the altars. The gargoyles are also a chapter in these books of stone, even though the translation of their chapter is encrypted and not easy to decipher.

In the Middle Ages, the older beliefs were still present. The day-to-day mythology of the people of Northern Europe was a blend of Christianity with Celtic, Nordic, and pagan legends, and was the rich folklore that formed the basis for the fairy tales that still frighten and amuse children today.

It is also always intriguing to speculate on the church hierarchy's reasons for allowing these little monsters to exist on a cathedral. Perhaps they were considered harmless because of their size and remoteness, or perhaps it was part of the subtle way that the medieval Church incorporated elements of deeply ingrained pagan culture in order to win the hearts and minds of the people.

Witch Gargoyle
Kölner Dom
Cologne, Germany
(Southwest corner, transept)
Nineteenth Century

▶

Donkey-Dragon Gargoyle
St. Pierre & St. Paul
Aumale, France
(South facade)
Sixteenth Century

The Time and Place of the Gargoyles

HATEVER the mythological environment into which they were born, the gargoyles were part of a major architectural revolution which drastically changed the physical environment of European cities. In the twelfth and thirteenth centuries, there were dozens of major building projects under way throughout Europe.

Gothic architecture evolved from the earlier, simpler Romanesque school and flourished from the twelfth to the early sixteenth centuries. As we have noted, the Gothic style began in, and spread from, northern France. As a style, it is seen as most typically characteristic of cathedrals and churches, although it is seen in many other buildings as well.

Technically, a Gothic cathedral or church is defined by its having a vaulted interior in which diagonal ribs are in direct conjunction with pointed transverse arches. In turn, the weight of the vaults as they push outward, is supported on the outside by arches known as flying buttresses. This design was revolutionary because it permitted construction of the largest and tallest enclosed rooms that the

Parapet Chimeras
Notre Dame de Paris
Paris, France
(North tower)
Thirteenth/Nineteenth Centuries

▶
Army of Gargoyles
Church of St. Séverin
Paris, France
(North facade)
Fifteenth Century

· · · · · · · · · · · · · · · · · ·

world had yet seen. These vast rooms were in contrast to the warrens of smaller rooms that characterized the architecture of earlier times. There are also many architectural details — including tall, narrow windows — that are characteristic of the Gothic style.

The first major Gothic building was the Abbaye Saint-Denis, completed near Paris in 1144. It was soon followed by the cathedral of Notre Dame in Paris, which still ranks as one of the architectural wonders of the world and an icon of Gothic architecture. Gargoyles, meanwhile, went little heralded, being relegated to their high and obscure portions of the cathedrals and churches. The great vaulted naves were meant to be experienced and the stained glass was meant to be seen, but the purpose of the grimacing little faces of the gargoyles is still unknown.

If the *time* of the gargoyles can be defined as the Gothic period in architecture — which reigned from the twelfth through the fifteenth centuries — then the *place*, or habitat range, of the gargoyles can best be explained as radiating from the area where Gothic architecture originated. This area centers on Paris, Chartres, and the Ile-de-France region, and it stretches north to include the ancient provinces of Normandy and Picardy in northeastern France. As the

Gothic style became international, gargoyles travelled to Germany, and across the channel to England.

The great cathedrals at Rouen in Normandy and Amiens in Picardy are inhabited by many splendid gargoyles, but so are many of the smaller parish churches throughout the area. The churches of Notre Dame at Louviers and St. Pierre & St. Paul at Aumale in Normandy are two excellent examples. Another is the Abbaye St. Ouen in Rouen, a building that is of the size and scale of a cathedral.

The Great Gothic Buildings

NOTRE DAME de Paris, probably the queen of all the Gothic cathedrals, is thought to have more gargoyles than any other Gothic building in the world. Including the well-known and much-photographed chimeras on the towers, there are no fewer than 500 gargoyles and grotesques. Notre Dame was begun in 1160, and its high altar was consecrated in 1182, although the famous towers were constructed between 1200 and 1245, a period to which art historians have dated most of the major ecclesiastical sculpture and statuary located around the cathedral's major portals. By the nineteenth century, Notre Dame and its gargoyles had fallen into disrepair, through both the wear and tear of time and the damage inflicted by the French Revolution in the 1780s.

Notre Dame's plight became a cause for Paris preservationists, led by Victor Hugo, whose 1830 novel *Notre Dame de Paris* — Revived in the twentieth century as *The Hunchback of Notre Dame* — evoked the lost wonder of Gothic art and architecture. Hugo's book was the catalyst that led to the first major restoration of a Gothic building. This project was carried out between 1844 and 1864 under the direction of the great French architect Eugene Emmanuel Viollet-le-Duc, who we have to thank for the current look of Notre Dame's spire as well as of its tower chimeras.

In 1232, work began on the chapel of Sainte-Chapelle in Paris, a structure constructed near Notre Dame on the Ile-de-la-Cité in Paris to house Jesus' crown of thorns, which King Louis IX had acquired (at great expense) from Emperor Baldwin II of Constantinople. At Sainte-Chapelle, the art of stained glass windows emerged as one of the glories of Gothic decorative art. On the exterior, the gargoyles blossomed, guarding — but forbidden to be near — the sacred relic.

Located 60 miles west of Paris, the cathedral of Notre Dame de Chartres is another legendary example of Gothic architecture. It is recognized as one of the

Pinnacle Gargoyles
Sainte-Chapelle
Paris, France
(Pinnacle, south side)
Thirteenth Century

Mask Gargoyles
Notre Dame de Chartres
Chartres, France
(Old [South] Tower)
Twelfth Century
· · · · · · · · · · · · · ·

world's most important architectural treasures, and is considered by many to be the most beautiful of the Gothic cathedrals — despite its mismatched towers. The older of these, and probably the oldest major extant component of the building, stands 350 feet high and was completed in about 1170. The 370-foot New Tower was designed by Jean Texier and completed in 1513. The gargoyles could not be more different. While those on the New Tower are reminiscent of other French gargoyles, those on the Old Tower have a strange, mask-

like character that reminds one of something that might be encountered in Japan, Tibet or on a Haida totem pole on British Columbia's Queen Charlotte Islands.

In Normandy, the cathedrals of Notre Dame de Rouen and Notre Dame d'Evreux are world famous architectural treasures, as well as being important gargoyle sites. Constructed between 1145 and 1250 and a favorite subject of impressionist Claude Monet, the Rouen cathedral is considered to be a time capsule of medieval art — from sculpture to stained glass —

because decorative embellishment continued into the sixteenth century. Among these are the fourteenth century tracery and statuary that were designed by Jean Perier in 1386. It is probable that his team included gargoyle sculptors, for gargoyles are certainly an integral part of the overall design of the tracery. The sculptural work at Notre Dame de Rouen also includes the well-regarded fourteenth century tympanum that is carved over the main entrance. One wonders whether the "Descent Into Hell" that is portrayed here may have been carved by the same sculptors who carved the gargoyles high above.

Also in Rouen, the regional Palais de Justice is a reminder that the habitat of the gargoyles is not limited to ecclesiastical buildings. This building, also remembered as the Ancient Parliament of Normandy, was completed in the last year of the fifteenth century. Although it was heavily damaged by twentieth century warfare, it still hosts one of the largest single collections of gargoyles in Normandy.

The largest cathedral in France, Notre Dame d'Amiens was part of the second generation of Gothic cathedrals that also included those at Laon, Noyon, and Senlis, all in Picardy. It was built between 1290 and 1375, with contemporary records indicating that the team of artisans involved was especially talented. This is especially true of the sculptural work in the tympanum of the Last Judgement that is located over the central portal on the west face between the towers — and of the gargoyles. Among the latter are perhaps the largest number of rabbits and other long-eared creatures to be found among gargoyles at any Gothic site. This is possibly due to the dense population of such mammals which inhabited Picardy in the thirteenth century.

Outside northern France, gargoyles are present, but less common. In the French-speaking parts of what is now Belgium, gargoyles are more prevalent than in the Flemish-speaking areas. In Antwerp Province, the cathedral in the city of Antwerp has none, while the fifteenth century cathedral of St. Rombout in neighboring Mechelen has an amazing collection of gargoyles. Gargoyles are sparse on the cathedral and churches at Brugge in West Flanders, but there are several commercial buildings in Brugge which are home to large groups of gargoyles. Among the most notable of these is the fifteenth century Burghers' Lodge (or Porters' Hall), that is located on Van Eyck Plein.

In Brabant — which extends to both sides of the present Belgium-Netherlands border — public build-

▲

Gargoyle Rookery

Notre Dame d'Amiens

Amiens, France

(Apse pinnacles)

Fourteenth Century

▶

Dragon Gargoyle

Burghers' Lodge

Brugge, Belgium

(South facade)

Fifteenth Century

· · · · · · · · · · · · · · · ·

ings also host numerous gargoyles. A case in point is Brussels, where the Hôtel de Ville (Town Hall) on the Grand Place is home to a striking collection of beasts that range from gruesome mermaids to hooded monsters with bulging eyes. The Hôtel de Ville was constructed between the thirteenth and fifteenth centuries, but the center of Brussels was sacked by the French in 1695, and restoration efforts — probably including the gargoyles — continued into the nineteenth century.

In the province of Noord Brabant (North Brabant) on the Netherlands side of today's international border, the cathedral of Sint Jan (St. John) in s'Hertogenbosch is a veritable wildlife preserve of gargoyles, and probably the densest concentration of them in the Netherlands. As discussed below in our section on gargoyle "species," this may have been related — more as a cause than as an effect — to the fact that s'Hertogenbosch was the hometown, at the end of the fifteenth century, of visionary painter Hieronymus Bosch.

In Germany, the most important Gothic cathedral — and the most important gargoyle rookery — is the Kölner Dom, the cathedral in the city of Cologne (Köln). Begun in 1248 on a site overlooking the Rhine River, the Kölner Dom was incomplete for

Loch Ness Monster Gargoyle
Town House
Inverness, Scotland
(South facade)
Nineteenth Century

Dragon Gargoyles
Westminster Hall
London, England
(Northwest tower)
Fourteenth Century

centuries, until a 60-year final push brought it to completion in 1880. It was, in turn, heavily damaged in World War II, so many of its gargoyles are twentieth century reconstructions of nineteenth century originals. As late as the 1990s, sculptors were still at work on huge new gargoyles (*see the picture on page 36*).

In Britain, as in Flanders and Germany, the gargoyle population is less dense than in northern France. With notable exceptions at places such as Oxford, York, and Lincoln, there were few gargoyles north of London until the Gothic Revival, when they appeared in many places throughout England and Scotland. One particularly notable Scottish gargoyle is the one on the neo-Gothic Town House in Inverness that some people have suggested may have been inspired by tales of the Loch Ness Monster.

In London, one of the most important collections of Gothic-era gargoyles and grotesques is that which adorns Westminster Hall, which was remodeled by Richard II in the 1390s. Gargoyles are rare at nearby Westminster Abbey, which was begun in 1245, but not completed until the sixteenth century. Adjacent to Westminster Hall, Britain's Houses of Parliament were constructed between 1840 and 1860 during the Gothic Revival, so one has the curious sight

of medieval gargoyles staring across a few dozen yards of cobblestones at Victorian gargoyles. Towering over Westminster, the 318-foot clock tower that contains Big Ben is an aerie of Gothic Revival gargoyles.

Rediscovering Gargoyles

BY THE fifteenth century, as the era of the great cathedrals was coming to a close, Gothic architecture was gradually being replaced by that of the Renaissance. New architectural ideas about the use of light and space drew on the classical — i.e. Greco-Roman — style that had been rejected by the medieval architects. In turn, the architects of the Renaissance — like their contemporaries in the fields of art and literature — rejected what they saw as the darkness and stiffness of Gothic style. Indeed, the very term "Gothic" was not used in the Middle Ages to describe contemporary architecture. It was coined as a derogatory term during the Renaissance — referring to the barbarian Goths — to describe medieval construction as being stiff, crude, and without any redeeming aesthetic qualities — In short, "ugly."

For the ensuing three centuries — as Renaissance style gave way to the Baroque, the Rococo and the Classic Revival eras in architecture — Gothic style was

▲

King Gargoyle
Kölner Dom
Cologne, Germany
(Exterior, south ambulatory)
Nineteenth/Twentieth Centuries
. . . .

considered obsolete and unfashionable. The gargoyles, meanwhile, remained on their perches, largely forgotten or ignored by architects.

At the beginning of the nineteenth century, the Gothic style returned. Just as the Renaissance had leapfrogged back in time to "re-discover" the classical, the Gothic Revival reached back to the Middle Ages. As a style, the Gothic Revival dominated much of the public building activity in Europe and the United States through the middle of the nineteenth century.

Among the architectural masterpieces of this period are the Albert Memorial in London, the Scott Memorial in Edinburgh, St. Patrick's Cathedral in New York, and the finishing work on the Kölner Dom in Cologne, which we have cited as home to Germany's most well-known gargoyle rookery.

The Gothic Revival in architecture was accompanied by an interest in what were seen as the pure Christian values of the Middle Ages, as represented by Gothic style. Just as there was a direct reaction to the Classic Revival architectural style popular in the eighteenth and early nineteenth centuries, there was a reaction to the humanist and perceived non-Christian values of classical thought.

Where did this leave the gargoyles? The architectural school that had allowed them to flourish was back,

Human Gargoyles
West Flanders Provincial Building
Brugge, Belgium
(West facade)
Nineteenth Century
. . . .

but there was no record of why the gargoyles were there originally — except as water spouts — or what all they represented. During the nineteenth century, the great vaulted ceilings and flying buttresses of the medieval cathedrals were well understood and highly praised as works of engineering, but the gargoyles were dismissed as a strange — and for some, embarrassing — mystery.

By the twentieth century, the gargoyles were no longer embarrassing. While their true iconography was — and is — largely unknown, gargoyles had now become icons of a popular culture that thrives on odd creatures and embraces everything from Boris Karloff as Frankenstein's monster and slippery aliens from Roswell to the menagerie that George Lucas and his colleagues have created for films such as *Star Wars*.

Each time that Victor Hugo's *The Hunchback of Notre Dame* has been adapted as a film, there have been the obligatory scenes in which the actor portraying Quasimodo is pictured among the legendary chimeras that exist at the real Notre Dame. The list of the little monsters' co-stars has been impressive: There was Lon Chaney in 1923, Charles Laughton in 1939, and Anthony Hopkins in 1982. In the 1996 Disney version, the stone figures were actually animated into supporting actors. Film and television, particularly in the B-movie genre, have always offered a welcome home to gargoyle-inspired "monsters" of various kinds. In the 1984 film *Ghostbusters*, the Gothic Revival gargoyles that grace Central Park West apartment buildings came to life to wreak havoc and mischief in New York City; while in 1994, the Buena Vista Television department of Disney began producing an animated television show called *Gargoyles*, in which gargoyles and grotesques came to life as crime-fighting good guys.

Gargoyle reproductions are also popular, especially in the souvenir shops adjacent to the cathedrals in Paris and Chartres. In the United States, such companies as Design Toscano in Arlington Heights, Illinois have been purveying reproductions of classic gargoyles, as well as those of original design, for home and garden.

Though they are no longer a common form of architectural decoration, during the twentieth century there were a number of gargoyles installed on important buildings. In the United States,

▲

Gargoyle Sculptor

Kölner Dom

Cologne, Germany

(Workshop)

Twentieth Century

▶

Steel Gargoyles

Chrysler Building

New York City, USA

(Main tower)

Twentieth Century

· · · · · · · · · · · · · · · · ·

these have included the Cathedral of St. John the Divine in New York City; the National Cathedral in Washington, DC; and Grace Cathedral in San Francisco. Gargoyles were also still a popular embellishment on commercial buildings through the first half of the twentieth century. New York still has hundreds of these modern relatives of Gothic classics, including those at the southeast corner of Madison Avenue and East 29th Street (*see page 10*). The most important of this genre, and probably the most famous twentieth century gargoyles, are, of course, the massive stainless steel art deco eagles that adorn New York City's landmark Chrysler Building.

As the twentieth century gave way to the twenty-first, the skill of the modern stone-worker has been employed in the carving modern replicas for medieval buildings. In the 1990s, there were huge new gargoyles being carved (*left*) for the Kölner Dom in Cologne, while in in Mechelen, Belgium, the firm of Natuursteen Vlaminck was at work on the restoration of St. Rombout's Cathedral. At Oxford in England, the masonry firm of Axtell Perry Symm continues to be actively engaged in carving gargoyles — as well as other architectural details — for buildings such as the famous Wolsey Tower (*see the pictures on pages 110 and 111*).

Species of Gargoyles

THE USE of animals as symbols in art is not unusual. We see it throughout the world, and it has been present in most world cultures for centuries. We see carved human, animal, and hybrid faces peering at us from high places in temples in Japan and from totem poles in Alaska. In Europe, decorative devices with animals such as lions and eagles have been common on religious and secular buildings since well before Roman times, and they are still used today. Statues representing real or mythological people are also a part of the design of buildings throughout the world during all historical periods.

Gargoyles are distinct from other statuary because of their typically bizarre and exaggerated forms, although many are are literal or variously stylized representations of natural species. As in painting, sculpture, manuscript illumination, and the decorative arts, these natural species are frequently used as symbolic icons. Lions and eagles represent bravery or royalty, while bears may be used to represent the ancient Celtic warrior class.

In ecclesiastical garb, animals are often a form of satire. Goats may be used to represent the devil, but at the Collegiate Church of Sainte-Waudru in Mons, the devil is also represented by a feathered, web-footed cow.

Gargoyle species are as varied as the species in the animal world which they mimic and parody. Meanwhile, many of the more memorable gargoyles are hybrids, including creatures that are half human and half animal, such as mermaids or dog-headed people. While many of the hybrids are primarily based on specific, recognizable, naturally-occurring species, many are strange and largely indecipherable.

Speaking of hybrids: as noted above, the greatest gargoyle rookery in what is now the Netherlands is located on the Cathedral of Sint Jan in the comfortably prosperous Dutch city of s'Hertogenbosch, the home of the master of hybrids in medieval painting, Hieronymus Bosch. Bosch lived and worked between 1480 and 1516, at a time when the Middle Ages were giving way to the Renaissance, and his work represented the mythology of the Middle Ages expressed in the relative freedom of the Renaissance. What relation Bosch may have had with the gargoyle sculptors has been debated for years. However, while finishing touches were being done to the cathedral in Bosch's lifetime, most of the gargoyles were probably carved many years before he was active.

▲
Devil Cow Gargoyle
Church of Sainte-Waudru
Mons, Belgium
(South apse)
Seventeenth Century

▶
Human-headed Monster
Cathedral of Sint Jan
s'Hertogenbosch, Netherlands
(South tower)
Fifteenth Century

In an informal demographic study of gargoyles throughout Europe, we have discovered that the most commonly represented mammal species are canine, feline, or hybrids that are mostly canine or feline. The former includes many wolves and fierce wolf-like dogs, but there are also gargoyles whose heads resemble lop-eared retrievers or hounds. Among the feline, most appear like domestic cats or European wildcats. When lions are represented, their manes are usually not prominent, and often are merely suggested. While the cats may represent cleverness or aloofness and dogs may represent loyalty, both species certainly represent the types of animals that were most often likely to be present on the construction sites as the cathedrals were being built.

Other common mammals that are often represented include rodents of various types and domestic animals, such as cows and pigs. Horses are rarely seen as gargoyles, perhaps because they figure in the large triforium and tympanum sculptures on the cathedrals and in heroic statuary. When goats are depicted, they are often in hybrid forms that suggest the devil.

Among gargoyles whose heads are definitely bird-like, many are certainly hawks or eagles, while some have enormous beaks that remind the viewer of a twen-

Bat-like Grotesque
Church of St. Séverin
Paris, France
(West portal)
Fifteenth Century

▶

Dog Gargoyle
Notre Dame d'Evreux
Evreux, France
(Exterior, south ambulatory)
Thirteenth Century
· · · · · · · · · · · · · · · ·

tieth century cartoon parody of a chicken. Smaller birds indigenous to Europe — such as swallows, sparrows, and songbirds — are almost never represented, but exotic species such as parrots are occasionally seen.

Bats, the largely misunderstood night-flying mammals that figure prominently (if inappropriately) in demonic iconography, are often invoked in the form and appearance of gargoyles. We say "invoked" because, while there are gargoyles that are literal representations of dogs, cats, and other animals, we almost never see a bat literally depicted as a gargoyle. On the other hand, the suggestion of leathery, bat-like wings is very common, and so is the depiction of large, bat-like ears on bat-like heads. There is a grotesque on the front of St. Séverin Church in Paris that appears to be exactly bat-like in its head and body until one notices that it has four legs and no wings.

Just as full representations of bats are far less common than hybrids that use bat parts, there are few gargoyles that represent recognizable reptiles, but many gargoyles that have scaly, reptilian skin or other reptilian body parts. Snakes or serpents, which figure prominently in medieval literature, are less common than a snake-like tail on a hybrid beast. At the Collegiate Church of Sainte-Wau-

dru in Mons, Belgium, there is that famous gargoyle that is a winged squirrel with a turtle's shell. (Or is it a turtle with a squirrel's head?)

The most common species of gargoyle — probably more common than even the canine or the feline types — is the completely fictitious hybrid. These are typically winged, dragon-like creatures with long claws. The wings are often bat-like, but they may just as well be feathered. The paws — or hands — are more like a bird's or reptile's than a mammal's. The faces of such gargoyles are mammalian, but are of indeterminate species. They seem a bit canine, a bit feline, and often bat-like. Most unnerving is that the expressions are often almost human. The ears are larger in proportion to the face than in most natural species, except in bats and certain breeds of dogs. Curiously, virtually all gargoyles that do not specifically incorporate birds' heads have ears of some kind. Even those that appear very reptilian have ears.

In considering the side by side mix of real and imaginary animals, it should be pointed out that the medieval bestiaries, the books which listed and pictured the animals of the world, included the real along with the fictitious with no distinction. Indeed, the imaginary animals often had a higher place

▲
Flying Squirrel-Turtle
Church of Sainte-Waudru
Mons, Belgium
(South apse)
Seventeenth Century

▶
Seal-tailed Chimeras
Notre Dame de Paris
Paris, France
(North tower)
Thirteenth/Nineteenth Centuries
· · · · · · · · · · · · · · · ·

in mythology than more mundane natural species. Among the mythological beasts in the bestiaries were the hybrids that had their roots in Greco-Roman folklore. Griffins, which are part lion and part eagle, are present throughout medieval mythology. They are still present as an important icon of heraldry, and occasionally as gargoyles.

The fearsome mythical chimera had a lion's head, a goat's belly and a serpent's tail. Homer discusses the legendary chimera in *Book VI* of the *Iliad* and Hesiod, writing in *Theogony*, describes it as breathing fire. While chimeras are occasionally seen as gargoyles, in France, the French word *chimére* is used almost a synonym for *gargouille*. The famous statues on the parapets at Notre Dame de Paris — which are usually referred to colloquially in English as "gargoyles" — are known locally as *chiméres*. While none of these actually depicts a classic chimera form, beneath the Notre Dame parapets there are some lion-headed creatures with vaguely serpent-like (or possibly seal-like) tails half-hidden in the limestone foliage.

The dragon is another mythological creature that plays an important role in European myth, folklore and bestiaries. There was a widespread belief in the existence of dragons, which were

generally portrayed as giant lizards with sharp claws, bad dispositions, and fiery breath. While no one had actually seen such a beast, the fact that its image was seen in bestiaries made it seem real. Today, as supermarket tabloids and magazines feature images of space aliens, a growing number of people have begun to believe that aliens too, are real. The superstition prevalent during the Middle Ages was once attributed to the lack of education, but the fact that nearly half the people in America today believe that space aliens visit the Earth shows that superstition is a part of human nature.

There seems to be something in human nature that wants to believe in creatures that we have never seen. Today, there is an elaborate folklore supporting the existence of such diverse creatures as the Roswell alien, the Loch Ness plesiosaur, the abominable snowman and his American cousin, the sasquatch or bigfoot. The same was true for medieval Europeans, many of whom believed that the hybrids described in folk tales, seen in illuminated manuscripts and bestiaries, or carved on cathedrals actually existed in nature. Many northern Europeans had never seen a camel, but most believed that they existed. If a camel existed in nature, why was it impossible for there to be unicorns or dragons?

Dragon Gargoyle
Notre Dame d'Evreux
Evreux, France
(Exterior, south ambulatory)
Thirteenth Century

The Basilisk Chimera
Notre Dame de Paris
Paris, France
(North tower)
Thirteenth/Nineteenth Centuries

. . . .

Two variations on the dragon theme that show up frequently as gargoyles are wyverns and basilisks. The basilisk is often, albeit not always, portrayed as a two-legged dragon or a two-legged snake. One of the *chiméres* on the parapet of the north tower at Notre Dame is known as *The* Basilisk.

In ancient and medieval mythology, the basilisk was believed capable of killing with a glance. This is a possible origin of the term "evil eye." The basilisk legend is also related to the Greek story of Medusa, the beautiful gorgon woman who turned into a hideous hag with an evil eye and serpents as hair. As with Medusa, basilisks were said to be defeated through the use of a mirror carried into battle against them. In this way, the deadly stare was reflected back upon the basilisk, killing it.

The historian Pliny the Elder, writing in the first century AD, described the basilisk as though he had actually observed it as a natural species: "Not more than 12 inches long, and adorned with a bright white marking on the head," he wrote, "it kills not only by its touch, but also with its breath, scorches up grass and burns rocks. Its effect on other animals is disastrous: It is believed that once one was killed with a spear by a man on horseback, and the infection rising

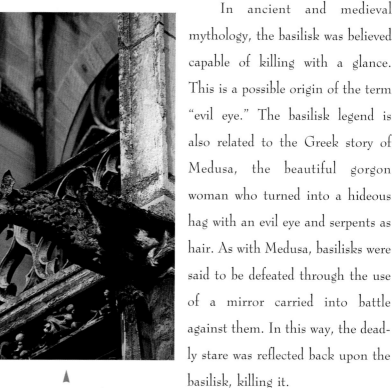

through the spear killed not only the rider but the horse." A fearsome creature indeed!

The basilisks, like the wyverns and other dragons, were often pictured as having leathery, bat-like wings, a characteristic which seems to be part of the anatomy of many other hybrid creatures portrayed in manuscript illumination and as gargoyles. Perhaps this characteristic was designed to underscore an evil connotation, as there was a widespread belief — "confirmed" in Dante Alighieri's thirteenth century *Inferno* — that the devil himself had leathery wings.

Some of the more striking and memorable gargoyles and grotesques were designed to embody physical characteristics that, in medieval iconography, were associated with the appearance of the devil. These included the leathery wings mentioned above, as well as a contorted face, a tail, and horns. The latter still figure in our cartoon/caricature images of the devil.

There are a large number of horned gargoyles, most with two horns, but a few with a single horn. Many of these have leathery, bat-like wings, so we can assume that the devil is being suggested.

As with the satyrs of classical mythology, the devil was often portrayed as being goat-like, with a goat's horns, tail, and cloven hooves. (Seeing tracks of cloven hooves in unusual places often suggested that one had

Green Man and Lion Grotesques
Westminster Hall
London, England
(West facade)
Fourteenth Century
. . . .

been visited by the devil.) Many of the horned gargoyles with generally human bodies have faces with features that are a blend of goat and human features.

Another curious creature present among the gargoyles and grotesques is the foliage-encrusted green man. The green man is of interest today because he is a prominent figure in the pre-Christian, pagan mythology which has been re-discovered and embraced by modern-day neo-paganists and believers of certain new age religions. He was also very popular in the Middle Ages. Louis Aubert sees the green man — or "vegetable gargoyle" — as demonstrating the preoccupation of the medieval philosopher-alchemist with nature.

The green man has gone by many names. In England, he has been called Jack of the Green ("Jack o' Green"), Jack of the Spring, and Jack Yule. He is usually pictured as a face with a playful smile surrounded by, or composed of, leaves and vines. As a symbol of the natural world, he originated in Greek legend, and is almost certainly associated with the great god Pan, the universal god of nature.

Among the green man's first cousins are the likes of Puck, Robin Goodfellow, the brownies, and even Rumpelstiltskin. All of them were playful, forest-dwelling, little men. Such characters are common to the folklore throughout northern Europe. They are

Jolly Devil

Cathedral of St. Rombout

Mechelen, Belgium

(Apse, southeast side)

Fourteenth Century

present in fairy tales, and Jack o' Green was revived in nineteenth century England to play a role in annual May Day celebrations.

It has been said that the green man embodies the essence of the spirit of the forest, representing the male aspects of the seasonal cycle of birth, death, and rebirth, just as the goddess Gaia — the Earth Mother — represents the female aspects of nature. For ancient people, and some people today, the green man helps to reveal nature's mysteries. Indeed, both he and the goddess are present in the annual May Day festivities, which celebrate the rebirth of life in the spring, perceived by ancient people as being one of nature's greatest triumphs.

Perhaps it is among the greatest complements to this belief that the Catholic Church associates Mary, the mother of Jesus Christ, with the Month of May. Like St. Patrick using established pagan iconography in his design of the Celtic cross, this is an example of the Church making itself relevant by designing its liturgy around that which was part of an established belief system.

Gargoyle Rookery (by day)
Notre Dame de Paris
Paris, France
(South tower)
Thirteenth/Nineteenth Centuries

The cultural historian Jules Michelet suggested in his early nineteenth century studies of medieval paganism and sorcery, that "The Church rejects nature as something impure and suspect. Satan seizes on it and makes it his pride and ornament."

While it is certainly true that the Church officially discouraged and even persecuted paganism, the people who brought Christianity to Northern Europe were probably far more accommodating on a practical level than the nineteenth century commentators believed.

Perhaps too, it is not ironic that in an era when the cathedrals were being erected to dizzying heights in order to be closer to heaven, the ingrained heritage of many average people was still tied to the Earth and forest. It may very well be that the presence of the green man and the strange mysteries of nature amid the spires of the cathedrals represented a comfortable accommodation. After all, the God that was being worshiped within the glory of the cathedrals was the creator of the natural world that the green man represented.

As the Lights Go Out

Gargoyle Rookery (by night)

Notre Dame de Paris

Paris, France

(South tower)

Thirteenth/Nineteenth Centuries

. . . .

THE art historian John Stocking once said that a Gothic cathedral is like a cave — rich in stalagmites and stalactites — turned inside out. Just as the formations within caves have the appearance of being living things, so too do the surfaces of the cathedrals and the gargoyles that live on those surfaces. cathedrals. The texture of the cathedral's surface is intricately and deliberately carved by human hands, yet when the cathedral is observed from a dis-

tance, it has the appearance of being a natural or organic environment. As the light is fades, one may often be fooled by the illusion of a flicker of movement in the midst of that architectural detail. This book is a tribute to these little known beasts that inhabit those caves turned inside out, and to the craftsmen who created them. As the lights go out, the gargoyles will stretch their stony necks, glance about and stare down at lively cities and sleeping villages as they have for eight centuries or so, their origins still comfortably obscure and mysterious.

THE PLATES

▲ **Gargoyle Rookery**
Sainte-Chapelle
Paris, France
(Pinnacles and southwest tower)
Thirteenth Century

► **Gargoyle Rookery**
Sainte-Chapelle
Paris, France
(Pinnacles at the southeast corner)
Thirteenth Century

◄ **Gargoyle Rookery**
Sainte-Chapelle
Paris, France
(Pinnacles at the southeast corner)
Thirteenth Century

▲
Jamb Gargoyles

Sainte-Chapelle

Paris, France

(South exterior wall of the nave)

Thirteenth Century

▶
Gargoyle Rookeries

Sainte-Chapelle

Paris, France

(South exterior wall of the nave, south-

west tower and the Spire)

Thirteenth Century

Dragon Gargoyles

Westminster Hall

London, England

(Northwest tower)

Fourteenth Century

Winged Lioness Gargoyle

Westminster Hall

London, England

(Northwest tower)

Fourteenth Century

Demonic Chimeras and Gargoyles

Notre Dame de Paris

Paris, France

(Southwest corner of south tower)

Thirteenth Century (but probably

restored in the Nineteenth Century)

Eagle Chimera

(Close-up view showing chisel marks)

Notre Dame de Paris

Paris, France

(Southwest corner of north tower)

Thirteenth Century (but probably

restored in the Nineteenth Century)

▲

Gargoyle Rookery

Notre Dame de Paris

Paris, France

(Top, southwest corner of the

south tower)

Thirteenth Century (but probably

restored in the Nineteenth Century)

▶

Frog, Long-eared, and Human
Gargoyles

Notre Dame de Paris

Paris, France

(South exterior wall of the nave)

Twelfth Century

▲
Buck-toothed Gargoyle

Notre Dame de Paris

Paris, France

(Lower section of the north exterior wall

of the nave)

Twelfth Century

▶
Basilisk Gargoyle

Notre Dame de Paris

Paris, France

(Lower section of the north exterior wall

of the nave)

Twelfth Century

Hybrid Monster Gargoyles
Cathedral of Sint Jan
s'Hertogenbosch, Netherlands
(Pinnacle on the south exterior wall of
the nave)
Fifteenth Century

Hybrid Monster Gargoyle
Cathedral of Sint Jan
s'Hertogenbosch, Netherlands
(Amid the triforium tracery
on the southeast face of the apse)
Fifteenth Century

▲ **Lean, Dog-like Griffin Gargoyle**
Notre Dame de Paris
Paris, France
(South exterior wall)
Twelfth Century

▶ **Frightened Dog Gargoyle**
Notre Dame de Louviers
Louviers, France
(Triforium on the south exterior wall of
the nave)
Fifteenth Century

▲
Vicious, Bat-eared,
Wild Dog Gargoyle
Notre Dame d'Evreux
Evreux, France
(Exterior of the south wall of
the ambulatory)
Thirteenth Century

▶
Dog Gargoyle
Abbaye de Cluny
(Musée National du Moyen-Age)
Paris, France
(Dormer, south facade, overlooking
the courtyard)
Fifteenth Century

Dog-like Gargoyle

Notre Dame de Chartres

Chartres, France

(East side of the New, or north, tower,

near the top)

Fifteenth Century

Dog-like Gargoyle

Kölner Dom

Cologne, Germany

(South tower)

Nineteenth Century (but probably

restored in the Twentieth Century)

▲
Perching Wolf Gargoyle
Cathedral of St. Rombout
Mechelen, Belgium
(Apse)
Fourteenth or Twentieth Century(?)

▶
Hooded Wolf Gargoyle
Kölner Dom
Cologne, Germany
(Amid the tracery on a pinnacle near the
buttresses supporting the ambulatory)
Nineteenth Century (but probably
restored in the Twentieth Century)

▲
Wildcat Gargoyle

Notre Dame de Paris

Paris, France

(Lower section of the north exterior

wall of the nave)

Twelfth Century

▶
Winged Cat Gargoyle

Burghers' Lodge

(Porters' Hall)

Brugge, Belgium

(South facade)

Fifteenth Century

▲
Lion Gargoyle
Notre Dame de Louviers
Louviers, France
(Triforium on the south exterior wall of
the nave)
Sixteenth Century

▶
Lion Gargoyle
Notre Dame d'Evreux
Evreux, France
(Pinnacle on the south exterior of
the nave)
Thirteenth Century

▲ Lion Gargoyle Clutching a
Human Head
Notre Dame de Chartres
Chartres, France
(Exterior north wall of the nave)
Twelfth Century

▶ Lion Gargoyle Clutching a
Shield, and a Lion Grotesque
Westminster Hall
London, England
(Window frame on the south facade)
Fourteenth Century

▲
Hippopotamus and Lion
Gargoyles
Notre Dame de Chartres
Chartres, France
(West facade of the north transept)
Thirteenth Century

▶
Bear Gargoyle
Notre Dame d'Amiens
Amiens, France
(South tower)
Fourteenth Century

▲
Cow and Goat Gargoyles
(Undergoing Installation)
Kölner Dom
Cologne, Germany
(At the intersection of the East Side of
the south transept and the south exterior
wall of the ambulatory)
Twentieth Century

►
Monkey Gargoyle
Notre Dame d'Amiens
Amiens, France
(On an arch on the north tower)
Fourteenth Century

Hooded, Fish-headed Gargoyle

Cathedral of St. Rombout

Mechelen, Belgium

(north exterior wall of the ambulatory)

Fourteenth Century

Fish Gargoyle

Abbaye de Cluny

(Musée National du Moyen-Age)

Paris, France

(South facade)

Eighteenth Century

▲
Long-eared Gargoyle
Notre Dame d'Amiens
Amiens, France
(Apse)
Fourteenth Century

▶
Long-eared Gargoyles
Westminster Hall
London, England
(Southwest tower)
Fourteenth Century(?)
(Probably more recent retrofits)

Long-eared Gargoyle

Notre Dame de Paris

Paris, France

(South exterior wall of the nave)

Twelfth Century

Long-eared Gargoyle above a Rabbit Grotesque

Notre Dame de Paris

Paris, France

(In a pinnacle on the southeast corner of the apse)

Twelfth Century

▲
Two-headed Devil Bird Gargoyle
Notre Dame de Louviers
Louviers, France
(Triforium on the south exterior wall
of the nave)
Fifteenth Century

►
Rooster Dragon
Notre Dame d'Evreux
Evreux, France
(South exterior of the nave)
Thirteenth Century

Parrot Gargoyle
Notre Dame d'Amiens
Amiens, France
(Apse)
Fourteenth Century

Parrot Gargoyle
Collegiate Church of Sainte-Waudru
Mons, Belgium
(Gable of south transept)
Seventeenth Century

Parrot and Dog Gargoyles
Notre Dame d'Amiens
Amiens, France
(Apse)
Fourteenth Century

Owl and Dragon Gargoyles

Westminster Hall

London, England

(Northwest tower)

Fourteenth Century(?)

(Probably a more recent retrofit)

**Owl and Dragon Gargoyles with
Human and Goat Grotesques**

Westminster Hall

London, England

(Northwest tower)

Fourteenth Century(?)

(Probably a more recent retrofit)

Hooded Monster Gargoyle and
Friend
Abbaye St. Ouen
Rouen, France
(South exterior wall of the nave)
Fifteenth Century

Hooded Gargoyle Sitting on a
Man's Head
Notre Dame de Rouen
Rouen, France
(North facade)
Fourteenth Century

Hooded Feline Gargoyle

Notre Dame d'Amiens

Amiens, France

(West Corner of the Sacristy)

Fourteenth Century

Hooded Simian Gargoyle

Notre Dame d'Amiens

Amiens, France

(Southwest facade of the Sacristy)

Fourteenth Century

▲
Hooded Gargoyle

Groot Markt Post Office

Brugge, Belgium

(West facade)

Nineteenth Century

▶
Hooded Gargoyle

(Same as above)

Groot Markt Post Office

Brugge, Belgium

(West facade)

Nineteenth Century

▲
Hooded Monk Gargoyle
Notre Dame de Paris
Paris, France
(Apse)
Thirteenth Century

▶
Hooded Bird Chimera
Notre Dame de Paris
Paris, France
(North tower)
Thirteenth Century (but probably
restored in the Nineteenth Century)

▲
Shouting Person Gargoyle
Sainte-Chapelle
Paris, France
(South tower)
Thirteenth Century

▶
Jester Gargoyle
Abbaye de Cluny
(Musée National du Moyen-Age)
Paris, France
(Dormer, south facade, overlooking
the courtyard)
Eighteenth Century

▲

Pair of Human Gargoyles

Abbaye de Cluny

(Musée National du Moyen-Age)

Paris, France

(South facade)

Fifteenth Century

▶

Human Gargoyles

Westminster Abbey

London, England

(North exterior wall of the nave)

Twentieth Century

▲

Gargoyle Rookery

The Great Tower, Magdalen College

Oxford, England

(Corner of the Tower)

Twentieth Century

Army of Gargoyles

Wolsey Tower, Christ Church

Oxford, England

(Seen here at Axtell Perry Symm

Masonry at Osney Mead, Oxford, after

completion, but prior to installation)

Twentieth Century

▲ s'Hertogenbosch Mannikins:
Woman, Bugler, Devil, Scribe,
and Griffin
Cathedral of Sint Jan
s'Hertogenbosch, Netherlands
(Flying Buttress on the south side)
Fifteenth Century

► s'Hertogenbosch Mannikins:
Goat, Web-footed Griffin, Wood-
carrier, Brick-layer, and Shepherd
Cathedral of Sint Jan
s'Hertogenbosch, Netherlands
(Flying Buttress on the south side)
Fifteenth Century

▲
s'Hertogenbosch Mannikins:
Monster, Eagle, Butter-maker,
Monkey with its Young, and Gill-
eared Monster
Cathedral of Sint Jan
s'Hertogenbosch, Netherlands
(Flying Buttress on the south side)
Fifteenth Century

►
s'Hertogenbosch Mannikins:
Drummer, Percussionist, Flute-
player, Blind Man, and Monkey
Cathedral of Sint Jan
s'Hertogenbosch, Netherlands
(Flying Buttress on the south side)
Fifteenth Century

▲
**Green Men Beneath a Gargoyle
with a Copper Tube in its Mouth**
Notre Dame de Chartres
Chartres, France
(North exterior wall near the intersec-
tion of the north transept and
the ambulatory)
Thirteenth Century

▶
**Green Man
(Vegetable Gargoyle)**
Notre Dame d'Evreux
Evreux, France
(South exterior of the nave)
Thirteenth Century

▲
Almost Human Gargoyles

Sainte-Chapelle

Paris, France

(Pinnacles at the southeast corner)

Thirteenth Century

▶
Green Man

(Vegetable Gargoyle)

Notre Dame d'Evreux

Evreux, France

(South exterior wall of the nave)

Thirteenth Century

Gargoyle Representing a Wild
Man Abducting a Person
Cathedral of St. Rombout
Mechelen, Belgium
(Apse)
Fourteenth Century

Gargoyle Representing a Man in
Medieval Costume
Kölner Dom
Cologne, Germany
(Pinnacle on the south side)
Nineteenth Century (but probably
restored in the Twentieth Century)

▲
Grotesque Representing a Dragon
and St. George Slaying a Dragon
Westminster Hall
London, England
(West facade)
Fourteenth Century

►
Statue of St. Genevieve with
Angel and Demon Grotesques
Notre Dame de Rouen
Rouen, France
(Bookseller's courtyard, adjacent to the
north portal)
Fifteenth Century
(Carved by Guillaume Pontifs, the stat-
ue once held a candle which was being
lit by the angel, while the demon tried to
blow it out)

▲ **Sun Grotesque and
Devil Grotesque**

Notre Dame d'Evreux

Evreux, France

(South exterior wall of the ambulatory)

Thirteenth Century

▶ **Devil Gargoyle with Fins**

Abbaye de Cluny

(Musée National du Moyen-Age)

Paris, France

(Dormer, south facade, overlooking

the courtyard)

Fifteenth Century

▲
Devil Gargoyle
Collegiate Church of Sainte-Waudru
Mons, Belgium
(Apse)
Seventeenth Century

▶
Devil Gargoyle
Collegiate Church of Sainte-Waudru
Mons, Belgium
(Apse)
Seventeenth Century

Devil Gargoyle

Collegiate Church of Sainte-Waudru

Mons, Belgium

(Apse)

Seventeenth Century

Devil Gargoyle

Collegiate Church of Sainte-Waudru

Mons, Belgium

(Apse)

Seventeenth Century

▲

**Gargoyle with One Horn
Identified as Representing the
Devil**

Notre Dame de Paris

Paris, France

(South side of the top of the

north tower)

Thirteenth Century (but probably

restored in the Nineteenth Century)

▶

**Chimera with Two Horns
Identified as Representing the
Devil**

Notre Dame de Paris

Paris, France

(West parapet of the north tower)

Thirteenth Century (but probably

restored in the Nineteenth Century)

▲
Devil Head Mask Gargoyles
Notre Dame de Chartres
Chartres, France
(Upper part of the Old [south] Tower)
Twelfth Century

►
Dog and Devil Gargoyles
Sainte-Chapelle
Paris, France
(Pinnacle at the southeast corner)
Thirteenth Century

▲

Demon Gargoyle
Notre Dame de Chartres
Chartres, France
(New [north] Tower)
Fifteenth Century

▶

Banshee
(Vegetable Gargoyle)
Notre Dame d'Evreux
Evreux, France
(South exterior wall of the nave)
Thirteenth Century

Goat Gargoyle

Notre Dame de Paris

Paris, France

(Lower section of the north exterior wall

of the nave)

Twelfth Century

Goat-headed Gargoyle

Cathedral of St. Rombout

Mechelen, Belgium

(North exterior wall of the ambulatory)

Fourteenth Century

Goat Gargoyles

Cathedral of Sint Jan

s'Hertogenbosch, Netherlands

(Apse)

Fifteenth Century

Long-necked Gargoyles

Tour St. Jacques

Paris, France

(Northeast side)

Sixteenth Century

Long-necked Gargoyles

Tour St. Jacques

Paris, France

(South corner side)

Sixteenth Century

Shovel-headed Gargoyle

Abbaye de Cluny

(Musée National du Moyen-Age)

Paris, France

(East facade, overlooking the courtyard)

Fifteenth Century

Shovel-headed Gargoyle with Serpent's Tail

Abbaye de Cluny

(Musée National du Moyen-Age)

Paris, France

(East facade, overlooking the courtyard)

Fifteenth Century

▲
Horse-Headed Dragon Gargoyles
Grace Cathedral
San Francisco, USA
(Turret at the base of the spire)
Twentieth Century

▶
**Two-Headed Gargoyle with Massive
Tubes in its Mouths**
Kölner Dom
Cologne, Germany
(Pinnacle located southeast of the intersec-
tion of the transept and the ambulatory)
Nineteenth Century (but probably restored
in the Twentieth Century)

Dragon Gargoyle

Palais de Justice

(Ancient Parliament of Normandy)

Rouen, France

(South facade overlooking the courtyard)

Fifteenth Century

**Eared, Large-beaked Gargoyle
Clutching a Rabbit**

Palais de Justice

(Ancient Parliament of Normandy)

Rouen, France

(South facade overlooking the courtyard)

Fifteenth Century

Yawning Dragon Gargoyle

Palais de Justice

(Ancient Parliament of Normandy)

Rouen, France

(East facade overlooking the courtyard)

Fifteenth Century

Large-eared Dragon Gargoyle

Palais de Justice

(Ancient Parliament of Normandy)

Rouen, France

(South facade overlooking the courtyard)

Fifteenth Century

▲ Leering Gargoyle

Palais de Justice

(Ancient Parliament of Normandy)

Rouen, France

(South facade overlooking the courtyard)

Fifteenth Century

▶ Weathered Gargoyle

Palais de Justice

(Ancient Parliament of Normandy)

Rouen, France

(East facade overlooking the courtyard)

Fifteenth Century

▼ Foliage-faced Gargoyle and Friend

Palais de Justice

(Ancient Parliament of Normandy)

Rouen, France

(East facade overlooking the courtyard)

Fifteenth Century

▲

Feathered and Weathered
Bat-eared Gargoyle

Notre Dame de Louviers

Louviers, France

(South exterior wall of the nave)

Fifteenth Century

►

Hybrid Griffin Gargoyle
Clutching a Small Dog

Notre Dame d'Amiens

Amiens, France

(The Sacristy)

Fourteenth Century

Dragon and Human Grotesques

Notre Dame d'Evreux

Evreux, France

(Door jamb, entrance on south side)

Thirteenth Century

Two Quasi-humorous
Grotesques Fighting
Notre Dame d'Evreux
Evreux, France
(Door jamb, entrance on south side)
Thirteenth Century

▲

**Fish-like, Bat-winged, Hybrid
Gargoyle**

Hôtel de Ville

Brussels, Belgium

(North facade)

Fifteenth Century (but probably restored
in the Nineteenth Century)

▶

**Gargoyle with Multiple Adam's
Apples, but Few Teeth**

Hôtel de Ville

Brussels, Belgium

(North facade)

Fifteenth Century (but probably restored
in the Nineteenth Century)

▲

Angry Griffin Gargoyle

Notre Dame de Paris

Paris, France

(Door jamb on the west facade)

Thirteenth Century (but probably

restored in the Nineteenth Century)

▶

Chimeras Overlooking the Seine

Notre Dame de Paris

Paris, France

(Balcony on the south side of the

south tower)

Thirteenth Century (but probably

restored in the Nineteenth Century)

▲
Griffin Gargoyle
Church of St. Remy
Amiens, France
(North exterior wall of the nave)
Sixteenth Century(?)

►
Griffin Gargoyle
Notre Dame de Paris
Paris, France
(Door jamb on the west facade)
Thirteenth Century (but probably
restored in the Nineteenth Century)

▲
Bat-eared Gargoyles
Cathedral of Sint Jan
s'Hertogenbosch, Netherlands
(Apse)
Fifteenth Century

▶
Bat-faced Gargoyle
Church of St. Pierre
Licroult, France
(South corner of tower)
Sixteenth Century(?)

▲ Hybrid Gargoyles Flanking a
King Playing a Zither
Notre Dame d'Amiens
Amiens, France
(Apse, base of the roof)
Fourteenth Century

► Hooting Gargoyle Clutching a
Reptile
Abbaye de Cluny
(Musée National du Moyen-Age)
Paris, France
(East facade, overlooking the courtyard)
Fifteenth Century

▲

Demon Gargoyle

Notre Dame de Chartres

Chartres, France

(New [north] Tower, near the top)

Fifteenth Century

▶

Large-eared Griffin Gargoyle

Astride a Human Infant

Notre Dame d'Amiens

Amiens, France

(Apse)

Fourteenth Century

Haunted-faced Gargoyle with
Water Jar
Church of St. Remy
Amiens, France
(North exterior wall of the nave)
Sixteenth Century(?)

Strange-faced Gargoyle
Kölner Dom
Cologne, Germany
(South facade of the south tower)
Nineteenth Century (but probably
restored in the Twentieth Century)

▲
Crocodile/Sea Serpent Gargoyle
Church of St. Remy
Amiens, France
(North exterior wall of the ambulatory)
Sixteenth Century(?)

▶
Angry Gargoyle
Notre Dame d'Amiens
Amiens, France
(North tower)
Fourteenth Century

▲
Beast Gargoyle Eating a Smaller Creature
Notre Dame de Chartres
Chartres, France
(South wall of Old [south] Tower)
Twelfth Century

▶
Hybrid Gargoyles
Notre Dame d'Amiens
Amiens, France
(Apse)
Fourteenth Century

Demon Gargoyles

Notre Dame de Paris

Paris, France

(Southeast corner of the top of the

south tower)

Thirteenth Century (but probably

restored in the Nineteenth Century)

Lurking Dragon Gargoyle

Church of St. Pierre & St. Paul

Aumale, France

(Behind the south tower)

Fifteenth Century

Long-necked Dragon Gargoyle

Church of St. Séverin

Paris, France

(North facade)

Sixteenth Century

Dragon and Human Gargoyles

Westminster Hall

London, England

(Pinnacle on the west facade)

Fourteenth Century(?)

(Possibly more recent retrofits)

Dragon or Basilisk Gargoyles

Verzekering Building

Brugge, Belgium

(Base of the tower)

Sixteenth Century

Dragon Gargoyles

Westminster Hall

London, England

(Pinnacle on the west facade)

Fourteenth Century(?)

(Possibly more recent retrofits)

Badly-eroded Dragon Gargoyle

Notre Dame de Chartres

Chartres, France

(New [north] Tower, near the top)

Fifteenth Century

Dragon Gargoyle

Notre Dame de Chartres

Chartres, France

(New [north] Tower, near the top)

Fifteenth Century

▲
Long-eared Dragon Gargoyle
Notre Dame de Chartres
Chartres, France
(New [north] Tower, near the top)
Fifteenth Century

►
Dragon Gargoyle
Notre Dame d'Evreux
Evreux, France
(South exterior wall of the ambulatory)
Thirteenth Century

▲
Dragon Gargoyle
Notre Dame de Louviers
Louviers, France
(South exterior wall of the nave)
Fifteenth Century

▶
Dragon Gargoyle
Church of St. Pierre & St. Paul
Aumale, France
(Top of the south exterior wall of the nave)
Fifteenth Century

▼ **Gargoyle Rookery with a Myriad of Species**
Notre Dame d'Amiens
Amiens, France
(West side of south tower)
Fourteenth Century

INDEX

. . . .

Griffin Gargoyle
Notre Dame de Paris
Twelfth Century

▼